DIVINE DESIGN

POETRY

Of the Heart and Soul

Joseph Cashman

978-1-915502-50-6 © 2023 Joseph Cashman

All rights reserved. No part of this book may be reproduced, stored in a retrieval system, or transmitted by any means, electronic, mechanical, photocopying, recording or otherwise without written permission from the author. Published in Ireland by Orla Kelly Publishing. Cover image by the author.

Orla Kelly Publishing
27 Kilbrody,
Mount Oval,
Rochestown,
Cork,
Ireland.

This book is dedicated to my family

Acknowledgments

I offer sincere thanks to my family, friends and all who contributed directly and indirectly in bringing my collection of poetry to print.

With a special word of thanks to Susan, my family and Orla Kelly for their unwavering support. Again, this book is a cooperative creation. I am deeply grateful to all who contributed and helped in their own unique way in placing the book in your hands.

About the Author

Joseph lives in County Waterford and enjoys walks in nature, sports of all kind and writing. Many of the poems in this book are inspired by the beautiful surrounding local areas and his family.

Contents

Acknowledgments iv
About the Author v
Lullaby Divine 1
Divine Design 2
Moorings 4
Starlight 6
Family 8
Fidelity 9
Songs 10
Sovereign Soul Divine 12
Bridges of the Eyes 13
Mother's Grace 14
Vale Divine 15
Presence of Love 16
Unknown To Known 18
Heavens are Awake 19
Crescendo 20
Reunion 22
Soliloquy 24
Links of Love 26
Beauty Sublime 27
Blessings 28
Grace of Time Divine 29
Two Swans 30
Rose Divine 32
Vision 34
Stepping Stones 35
Love Aligned 36

All Is Prepared 37
Round Table Divine 38
Coming Ashore 39
New Dawn 40
Seeing 42
Grace of Love Divine 43
Heartfelt Wishes 44
Now 46
Garden 47
Completion 48
New Future Life 50
Please Review 51
Other Books by the Author 52

Lullaby Divine

All of the sands of time
Wash up on the shores
Of Divine's infinite love
That beckons the heart
To rest there with soul
As soul softly sings
A lullaby Divine.

And every note
Echoes lovingly
In soothing waves
Upon heart's memories
And remembrance of the song
That builds a bridge from the heart
To soul and infinite love of the Divine.

For heart and soul to stand upon
Or cross to the shores of infinite love
And return to moments in time
With the gentle melodies
Of lullaby Divine.

Divine Design

Divine design soars from Heaven's door
And swoops over highways of the heavens
Bringing the gifts of Divine that design the All
With Creator's Light and infinite Love Divine
To bestow upon the Earth and all of life below.

Where Creator's gift of light and infinite love
Pour upon our humanity in gentle waves of joy
And flow through our kind loving heart and soul
To bless our daily lives with special moments.

From simple acts of sharing with those we love
To friends that bless us with their loving kindness
And oft' times when paths cross just by chance
Surprising us with special moments or a helping hand
That show we are always loved and cared for
As we naturally share from a loving heart
And bless each other's day.

While some simple caring acts sweep across,
To others who see the act of loving kindness
That gift their lives with the joy of knowing
Other's care without expecting in return
From their human family who received.

And many a gift descends on rolling foam
As Divine Design soars over Earth below
To bless teeming seas and shores

With shoals of fish and fertile waters
And to bestow infinite abundance on nature's gardens fair
Where gentle deer quietly graze lush woodland verges
To sounds of buzzing bees on nearby fragrant flowers
Flapping busy wings and sipping on nature's nectar.

While sun's bright light shines from above
Refreshing all below with its warm caress
As Creator's infinite light and love
Bless Earth all life and humanity endlessly.

Moorings

The moorings of the berthed bounty are now secured
Of those who sailed upon the seas of life
Now safely home to their loved one and the land
To step upon the shores of life and leave the old,
Lapping on the quayside, to fall away with the tide.

While hands are clasped and arms embrace
To begin a brand new story
Welcomed home to solid ground
Where ample bounty is spread upon the table
To share their love and blessings of the land.

And many a tear of joy falls freely from their souls
That speaks a thousand words through eyes that meet
As they gaze upon the beauty of this time
Where every morsel that pass beyond their lips
Touch the taste buds of the soul
With infinite delight nourishing the body and heart alike
And nurturing the love now home to stay.

Where every floor is swept afresh
To prepare for the birth of dreams
In the hearts that meet
And don the garment of fidelity
As every pulse of heart's desire
Sends waves of love
Across the threshold of their lives
To bless their time together.

As time apart now passes into distant memory
Clearing more space between their hearts and souls
And building new bridges in present time
To a life that is now dreamed into being.

In each gesture that is filled with endless possibility
And choices blessed in cooperation's hand
That mirrors and multiplies as it gathers pace
Planting new seeds to blossom forth,
Upon the fresh horizons before their eyes
Where every moment fulfills, the yearnings of their love.

Starlight

Every line of roses growing in the land
Is bedecked with endless beauty
As night's starlit skies
Shimmer from above.

And every flower
Creates a rose profound
While swirling speeding starlight
Streams across the vast cosmic skies
From timeless lands and nameless galaxies
Whose names are written in the Heart of Love
As they travel to the jewel of many galaxies
To shine on Earth's lines of roses in the land.

Now fulfilled after journeying through eons of time
Past clouds of stars spanning the cosmic heavens
That sang songs to the swirling speeding starlight
In joyful tones of loving praise and remembrance
Of planet Earth's shining beauty beyond compare.

While all is overseen by Creator's Heart of Love
Whose infinite grace, light and endless love
Bless all life and the Earth forever more.

Family

A new life is born
And welcomed in
As the table is set
For one and all
Who share in the joy
Of our family blessings.

Where all are loved
And honoured within
Hearth and home
As all the yearnings
Dreams and visions
Are nurtured to blossom
In fertile ground.

While every wish
Spins a joy filled web
That bless all
When a wish fulfills.

And each meal
Shared together
Feeds the body
Soul and heart alike
That spirals into
Every facet
Of our family life.

Fidelity

With love swept hand
A wish is made
As all is gathered
Into one
In the flame of love
And fidelity.

Where a heartfelt wish
Is kindled afresh
As fidelity shines
It's brightest flame
Upon the wish made.

And all unspoken
Comes home to rest
In the bosom of their love
Where all is born anew
In the flame of fidelity.

To bless a moment
In their lives
With a wish fulfilled.

Songs

Songs are now remembered
That source from Emerald shores
And beckon the heart and soul
To lovingly create
With Mother's gentle hand.

And sing anew on pristine lands
The melodies of Creator's Love
To fill the garden green
Once more
With grace and beauty
And Emerald tones,

Colouring the Earth
And God's Divine blue skies
With Creator's Divine songs
From Heaven's Divine domain.

Gently filling the vessels
Of our hearts and souls
With Divinely inspired
And light-filled symphonies.

To bless the heavens, Earth
And every one
With love Divine's
Greatest symphonies.

Sovereign Soul Divine

Sovereign soul Divine reigns on high
And guide the journeys of its children forth
Through sunlit speckled dale and rolling hills
To treks across soaring snow-capped peaks
Where vistas span the heavens above
Making their journeys all worthwhile.

While every step is over lit by the love and grace,
Flowing from the heart of sovereign soul divine
Whose every heartbeat echoes lovingly
Across the hilltops and valley floors below.

Lighting beacons and signposts everywhere
For its children to journey onto higher ground
And connect with sovereign soul's gentle knowing
To guide each journey and fill their lives
With the blessings, love and grace
Of sovereign soul's caring heart
On the pathways of today.

Bridges of the Eyes

Rivers of Light flow through the eyes
That mirror realities in front and within
To grace the senses and join as one
Vistas that span the solid and the soul;

Where the sensory bridges of the eyes
Join thoughts to reason within the realm of mind
And heart with soul to touch the infinite and Divine
Igniting the emotional currents in the rivers of our light
That travel the limitless vistas of the solid and the soul
And journey beyond the boundaries of memory and time.

Returning with knowing that feel the information in light
To share with the landscapes of our waketime reality
Spanning the visible and invisible horizons of our eyes
And open new pathways from inner to solid outside.

As the sensory bridges before and within our eyes
Make sense of the information in the light
Mind, heart and soul lovingly create in harmony
New vistas and landscapes to grace our life.

Glistening with light and multicoloured love
Within the solid and subtle in time's terrain
And realms of the heavens Divine above
That add more letters and love
To the Alphabet of the Divine,
The language of light and love.

Mother's Grace

On a palette clear and filled with light
Divine Mother's Grace pours a Love profound
Upon the vessels of an Earth renewed
Sparkling with the colours of Her Love.

And all the Heavens is now awake
Filling the firmament with Her music
That emanates from
Her Sacred Heart Divine,
Joining the Heavens with the Earth
In perfect symphony and harmony
And everybody is replenished afresh
With the tones and colours of Her Love,

As She bestows Her benevolence
Upon all creation in Earth's domain
On land, sea and sky above
Where every colour flows as One
From the Presence of Her Love
That pours upon a blessed Earth
For ever more.

Vale Divine

Sacred sounds sweep across a vale Divine
On wings of love and light-filled symphonies
To bless the land and mountains high
With Holy Mother's grace and providence.

Where every stream reflects Her grace
Bestowed upon their sparkling waters
And every gateway in Divine's domain
Is open wide now for ever more
To fill the rose and every blossom too
With love and light Divine's great symphonies.

And every vessel in this green and fertile land
Is filled with Holy Mother's benign benevolence
That nurtures all of life and nature's kingdoms fair
With Infinite Love from Her Sacred Heart Divine.

As Her every wish awakens now to be fulfilled
On vale Divine and all beyond the furthest hills
That links with lands across the sea, once again
In Divine alignment and fulfils a Divine destiny.

Presence of Love

With caress Divine the touch of love
Embroiders every facet of our life together
And weaves a tapestry with finest silken touch
That spin on gossamer threads of infinite joy
With gentle benevolence and a warm soft caress
As familiar as the softest wafting summer's breeze.

Rekindling the resting passions of the heart and soul
In fond remembrance and recall of all our love
Through every moment of each unfolding season
Where every gentle glance and kiss of joy divine
Creates a carefree web of beauty and tranquillity
Within the vessel of our life and deepest longings.

While every word, feeling, deed expands our love
Endlessly, upon the furthest horizons of our lives
As bonds of trust blessed with simple caring acts
Echo along the shorelines of the Heaven's Divine
With softest tranquil sounds and soothing calm.

And come ashore in the heartland of our home
Where every threshold welcomes at the door
As table is set for nurturance without demand,
Round a loving circle of gentle abundant grace
Beside a warm hearth of care and cosy calm
Bestowing its flickering dancing flames
To all that rest beside its joyful dance
And beckon loving hearts to blessings
Pouring in from Heaven's open door.

Unknown To Known

All the pathways
Of the heart and soul
Come into view,
As all the ravelling
Comes undone.

And all that beckons
Heart and soul to know
Slides from unknown
To known.

As all the yearnings
Are now fulfilled
In the light of love
And the heart on high
To guide the way.

And every stepping stone
Shimmers with glints of gold
Along the pathways of the soul
And heart's terrain
Where every signpost
Is filled with starlight
To guide the journey
For ever more.

Heavens are Awake

All the Heavens are awake
With the light of countless suns
That span the breath of Earth's starlit skies
And their music fills the space within a vast arena
As all their symphonies sing songs in praise
Of the infinite light and love Divine
Blessing all of Earth below.

And every star filled wish
Descends from the firmament
Bathed in the tone of love Divine
To kiss the earthen skies, land and sea
With the golden glory of a new time blessed
While every starlit canopy fulfils the promises,
Made long, long ago with infinite love
To return to a long lost friend
And ring the Heavenly bells
Of love's remembrance
Across Earth's terrain
For ever more.

Crescendo

Since the dawn of time
Divine's light shines
From Heaven's shore
And steadily rose
To its ultimate crest,
In a roaring crescendo.

Of light's flight
On the cresting wave
Of love's journey
To the homeland shores
Of our heart's domain.

To be as one
In our heart's domain
And mirror the miracle
Back to the Divine.

And when
Light and love
Has made heart
It's home.

Love flows forth
Effortlessly
And travels
Everywhere.

In pulsing waves
Upon the light
With every beat
Of heart.

And all returns
To heart's domain
Softly laden
With a gift sublime
For the fertile soil
Of love and light.

To grow a pearl
Of priceless hue
That opens the heart,

To one another.

Reunion

They meet again
On the shoreline
Of their lives
Where footprints
In the sand
Join as one
On paths that cross.

Where memories
Of times before
Arise from the heart
With exquisite ease
And benign care.

That remember
Old parting paths
Now dissolving
Beneath the gaze
Of love's reunion
Shining from
Eyes embrace.

To join their circle
Once again
And create afresh
On new horizons.

As hands are held
In eternal knowing
That love is now

Home to stay
Within their heart's
For ever more.

Soliloquy

Divine's Heart on high
Many jewelled crown
Rests easy
In the light of love
And every jewel
Sings in soliloquy
With love's adornment
And Heaven's delight.

While every beat
Of Divine's Heart on high
Sends a stream of love
To share with all,
On its journey forth.

To all the stars
And our Sun alike
Who shares
It's love and light
With all the Earth
From deep blue sea
To hovering hummingbird.

Till journey's end
Rests upon
Our heart's
And soul's delight.

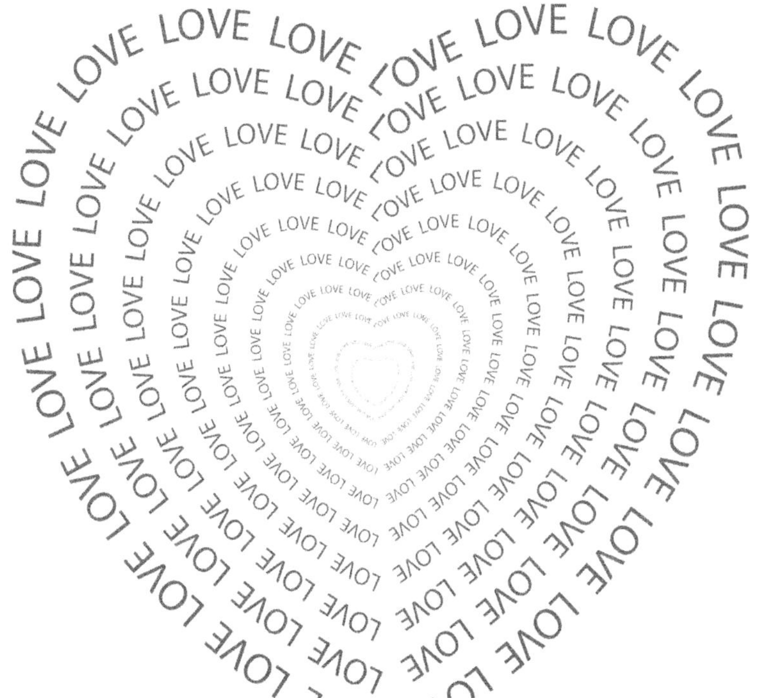
LOVE

Links of Love

Links of love
Flow to the Earthly realm
From Divine dwellings
And are mirrored
From the Heavens above
As the skies
Kiss the horizon of the eyes
Like the sea washes upon the sand.

And all is fashioned
In love's domain
Where all is given
In exultant joy,
To bless the beauty in our lives
With the silken threads of eternity
And every cell with abundant life.

That communicate with the heart and soul
In a language known and felt
Whispering gently through the voice of love
To link the words to our lips
Fulfilling the journey of creation forth
Bathed in the tone of love.

Beauty Sublime

On the fringes of many heavenly galaxies
Lies a planet Earth of beauty sublime
That is blessed by a billion stars and more
Around it's beautiful celestial dome
Who shine their shimmering light
On planet Earth's beauty beyond compare.

While sister Sun fill Earth's blue skies
And all below with clear bright light
As it's rays unfold the beauty everywhere
Across land and sea and, bubbling stream
On rolling hills and valleys too,

To soaring mountain tops with snow-capped peaks
That span the breath of Earth's horizons
Adorned with sunsets and rises of multicoloured love
While Divine creations soar on wings of joy
As life basks in the abundance far below.

And Earth's blue seas reflect upon the firmament
That sends a glow of love to Divinely realms
Resting up above and watching over all
And sees the seas wash upon the shores
Along the sands of time and tide
Where every season links in unison
And every atom is filled with Creator's love
In a never ending stream from our Heavenly home.

Blessings

Blessings abound in beautiful ways
And in many different guises to bless our lives
Oft' times on unexpected miraculous wings
That find a way to glide to our door
And land upon the hands of time.

With messages of love and grace-filled gifts
Where all is freely given without demand
Lifting and beckoning our hearts and souls to soar
And take that step on the journey of life
To greet the gifts unfolding before our eyes
Gently opening our heart to believe in blessings
Completing the circle of receiving what's given.

While many a gift filled with surprise and delight
Arrive in stages and serendipity sublime
Through people and places and paths that cross
By pure chance aligned with happenstance.

Where all springs from Divine's pure love for us
Awaiting in grace to find the right place
Within the tapestry of our daily life
To be spun and weaved with love and light Divine
Bringing beauty and joy to our days and nights.

Grace of Time Divine

Hands of time Divine
Arrive timeless from the Heavens
And pause no moment in their flight
On the wings of inspiration and delight
Alighting on the spiralling highways of the soul
And landing gently on the pathways of the heart.

Where every gateway on the pathway opens wide
To the timeless and infinite Grace of time Divine
Lovingly blessing our heart's and soul's
Every wish and deepest longings
That blossom effortlessly
Within the fertile soil
Of the Love flowing
From, the Heart
Of time Divine.

Two Swans

They came from on high
Like the winged Pegasus
From places unknown
To the human eye
That tell their story
Of days of yore.

With graceful
Remembrance
And love benign
As the two swans
Skim the waters
With their mighty wings
And webbed feet
To bridge the Earth
With the star-filled skies.

And many a tale
That goes unsaid
Is held in their hearts
And souls alike
As they land upon
The waters
And close their wings
To rest for awhile.

And when the time has come
Their souls and hearts ignite
The flame that stands
Between them

Of everlasting love
That transcends
The depths of time
And join their hearts forever
To be as One
With each other.

Rose Divine

Grace of a rose Divine
Blooms upon the awakened lands
In myriad ways and countless places
As every petal unfolds
Upon a destiny Divine.

And every blaze of Sun's bright rays
Unfolds the petals a little more
With exquisite ease and synchronicity
Across verdant vales and hillsides.

To bless the lives of everyone
And fill their hearts and more
With the grace of a rose Divine
Opening petals in heart's domain
To unfold a destiny Divine.

In full alignment with heartfelt wishes
That wash upon soul's terrain
Where every step of the journey home
Is blessed by the grace of a rose Divine.

Vision

A vision is now fully formed
From a heartfelt wish
And Heaven is pouring all
Through an open doorway
To touch and taste
In our reality,

With the swiftness
Of a swallow
That swoops in
With graceful remembrance
Of a home already prepared
For family, love and fidelity.

And every move
Is filled with love
As all flows effortlessly
Into our life together.

Where all is blended
Into one
As we live the vision
Into wholeness
With joy and laughter
And love profound.

Stepping Stones

Stepping stones of Divine design
Are built with love and Divine's great light
And hover in a space of timeless eternity
Awaiting the heart, mind and soul's request
To pour the stone upon the face of time.

And all is prepared
With gentle love and pure intent
That set aside the laws of time
Where all is fashioned with Divine's benevolence
Within the creative heart of highest soul-self
Creating the stone with synchronicity sublime.

That bless the stepping stone with gifts and grace
And creativity that opens doorways in the land of time
To welcome reflections of the stone in time's terrain
Mirroring the Divine design of the stone;

Through shapes in form and happenstance calling
And the many other ways of Divine's endless ingenuity
That guide the receptive heart to the completed stone,
Where all awaits in love's timing and light's illumination
That unite as one to place the stepping stone
Beneath the feet, to step upon Now.

Love Aligned

An all-new dawn
Has now arisen
As love Divine
In all its form.

And lo behold
The beauty born
With exquisite grace
Wrapped in the warmth
Of the undying flame.

As every mirror
Reflects the wholeness
Of our love aligned
To connect us now
For all of eternity.

All Is Prepared

All is prepared
In love's domain
For both to make
The journey home.

While each beacon
Lights the way
To the last step
And hearts embrace.

And every path
That led them home
Has now rolled up
Into one
For both to walk
In unison.

As dreams
And hearts
Come home to rest
On a new journey
Now unfolding.

Round Table Divine

Round table Divine where all are blessed and equal
And every placement bestows a welcoming grace
As each sit in gentle poise and are honoured there
While vales of bounty slope gently to the coast
And simple moorings lie softly on the sand
For boats that journeyed from afar
As highest sun on summer tide
Bless the sea and pristine shores.

And every hand on the table rests easy there
As hands are softly clasped in prayerful pose
To lovingly bless the endless beauty
Of Creator's hand on land and sea.

While at the table the bountiful is amply shared
As all is passed in one circular loving link
Like the countless stars around Earth's spherical home
That bless the lands and waters that Creation blessed.

As emerald Earth and sister Sun bloom bounty everywhere
While buzzing bees gather nature's light-filled nectar
And joyfully leave their passing gift of future fertility
Where all is one under God's Divine blue skies
As time touches the timeless and Divine.

Coming Ashore

Waters of Divine Light and Love
Lap gently on Emerald shores
That rises now from a slumber deep
To taste the freshness of a light-filled dawn
And bless the lands and life once more
Where every promise made and kept
Is coming ashore.

And every step taken
Upon the golden sands of time
Is now complete.
As light and love and, all Divine
Walks upon the hallowed lands.

While every footstep echoes deep
Awakening all to the Divine
That beckon hearts and souls
To breathe once more
Upon the fertile lands of Emerald fair.

Where Divine blesses all
From butterfly wings to sweeping valley floors
And rushing mountain streams, lakes and rivers
While waves wash gently onto Emerald shores.

And everyone is regent royal
In the graces and blessings of the Divine
Who reigns upon their lands and seas forever more.

New Dawn

On nearby cosmic skies
Divine's Light before the dawn
Sweeps across the starlit skies
To descend upon the firmament
In sparkling light and sacred symphonies
And sweep across Earth's awakening lands.

That mirror back the joy to the Heavens
In welcoming the bright new dawn
And bridge the star-filled skies
With the rolling hills and vales
To birth the Light
Of Divine Love's new dawning.

Seeing

In love's domain
The I remains but one
While the rivers of love
Reflect as two
Within a lover's eyes
To join again, as one
In heart and soul.

Where every sup
Drank from this cup
Join hands and heart
And soul
In sweet refrain.

As seeing in love
Remembers all melodies
Of heart and soul
That soar from human
To Divine.

And back to rest again
In love's embrace
As all the realms
Join as one
In a never ending
Stream of love.

Grace of Love Divine

Grace beneath our feet
Provide the sacred stepping stones
To converge our paths the day we meet
And move the mountains in between
Our hearts and souls Divine.

As every kiss of love's first glance
Soars our souls in ecstasy
In fond remembrance and recall
Of the love we shared before.

And every word we speak
Echoes through the canyons of our souls
That resounds upon our heart's domain
Flowering in Divine alignment land.

And all the Grace of Love Divine
Flows up from beneath our feet
To meet our first embrace
And join as One before our eyes
In love forever more.

As every stepping stone now join as one
Upon the pathway of our souls
That merge in Divine alignment
With our flowering heart for eternity.

Heartfelt Wishes

As the brightest Sun
Shines in the sky
It's countless rays
Nurture all
And new beginnings
Flourish everywhere
As hearts in blossom
Find each other.

Where every word
Between them
Echoes on the soul
Opening their hearts
To a love renewed
And rekindled forever.

While Heaven pours
It's gifts and grace
Upon their hearts
And souls
As every embrace
Unfolds their love
Across the threshold
Of their heartfelt wishes
Now being fulfilled.

Now

On the path of the present moment
The leaves of limitation are swept aside
And every leaf is scattered to the wind,
Casting limits waiting in the future
To one side, to create anew in every now.

Building life afresh in every moment
Upon the synergy of heart and soul's creativity
Creating upon the emotional crest of positivity
And mind's envisioning with intent
To mould their dreams, wishes and intentions.

Where all is placed upon the table
Of Divine's benevolence
And nurtured to fruition
In the creative heart
Of soul's highest self
And Creator's manifesting hand
To grace life's journey
With dreams, wishes and intentions fulfilled.

Garden

In Earth's domain
Morning's light
Shines on
Nature's gardens
Bedecked with flowers
That hang in graceful
Regal state.

As every colour
Adorns their coat
With shimmering hues
And the light
Of a new dawn
Now in its zenith.

While every ray
Of sun's bright light
Sweeps across
Blossomed gardens
Now sparkling bright.

And every pulse
In Earth's domain
Remembers
Every flower,
Each by name.

Completion

And now
The robes of glory
Are complete
As the light of love
Rises over the horizon.

And soul's
Many faceted-self
Sweep across the sky
And come home to rest
In a robe complete.

Where all the love
Embroidered within
Brings completion
To the greatest quest
In love's domain.

To join as one
Our many facet selves
On the spirals of our soul
As every spiral
Comes home to rest
In the journey
Of our life.

New Future Life

As I intend to stand with love
Upon the shorelines
Of my creating gift within
A journey of discovery begins;

Uncovering the knowing of the self,
That as I use the gift of my creativity
With pure intent and positivity
To shape my future with gentle care
I become the futurer creator of my life.

Fashioned by the heart, mind, emotion and soul
Within the creative heart of my highest soul self
Where my new futurer life begins to birth into form;

As I walk along the pathways of tomorrow
To meet my newly created future in solid form
Blessing life anew with creations fulfilled.

Please Review

Dear reader,

I hope you enjoyed my collection of poems 'Divine Design.' It would be most appreciated if you could spread the word so others may find my poetry and also if you can leave a review if you bought the book online.

Thank you.

Joseph

Other Books by the Author

Family and Love Poems is an uplifting and inspiring collection of poetry that celebrates the beauty of family and love. Richly illustrated and offering an array of positive insights, readers will be taken on an emotional journey full of meaningful moments.

Through this book, you will explore the special place family holds in our lives, the joys of love, the blessings of relationships, and more.

Each poem is overflowing with colourful imagery and heartwarming emotions. Not only will it touch the heart, but also inspire curiosity and invite you to reflect on the many facets of love.

Let this book be your guide to discovering all that life has to offer and truly appreciate its joys and depths. Find solace in the words of Family and Love Poems and create lasting memories to cherish for a lifetime.

Introducing 50+2 POEMS Just For You, a unique collection of original poetic works crafted to inspire and awaken the imagination. This special anthology includes over fifty poems covering numerous topics of interest that appeal to all ages.

With thought-provoking and inspiring reflections woven into each work, this delightful collection will bring a smile to your face and captivate you with its vivid imagery.

Each poem is written with emotion and vibrant detail to stir your senses. Let these words soothe your soul - fill your spirit with joy - spark the inner flame that ignites creativity.

Whether you're in need of a bit of personal motivation or want to share an inspiring poem with someone special, 50 + 2 Poems has something for everyone.

So come and enjoy an enchanting journey through each poem and make some magical moments with 50+2 POEMS - Just for You.

www.ingramcontent.com/pod-product-compliance
Lightning Source LLC
Chambersburg PA
CBHW041310110526
44590CB00028B/4314